19 Tips
for Starting Over Single

by RJ Thesman

Unless otherwise noted, Scripture quotations in this book are taken with permission from the Holy Bible, New American Standard Version®, Copyright©1960 by The Lockman Foundation, La Habra, California 90631

19 Tips for Starting Over Single

© 2013 RJ Thesman
ISBN-13:
978-1494388454

ISBN-10:
1494388456

Published in cooperation with GateWay of Hope
815 S. Clairborne, Ste 200
Olathe, KS 66062
913.393.GATE (4283)
www.GWHope.org

Printed in the United States of America

Introduction:

You're Starting Over Single and wondering how to not only survive; but also thrive. You want some sort of survival guide but at the same time, you don't want any cutesy answers or pathetic sympathy.

You just want to go forward in life, forget the past and learn how to live again – with joy.

You've already gone through some counseling and a group relationship where you met other singles. You've worked through the initial shock and listened to lots of advice. But somehow, you still feel a bit stuck.

You may feel like you're in SOS mode. Help! I'm Starting Over Single. Now what?

So what are some tips you can utilize that will help you move forward? What are some tried and true best practices?

The following **19 Tips for Starting Over Single** offer some practical ideas you can begin to implement right now. You might want to focus on one tip per week, either individually or with a group of friends who are Starting Over Single.

These tips are useful for whatever type of SOS status you're in: divorced, widowed or moving out of a long-term relationship.

Each of the tips is followed by **Action Points.** These are questions to help you process that particular tip and/or practical ideas you can use to implement that tip. Again, you can work on this individually or with a group of friends.

So pull up a comfy chair and relax.

You're on a journey and you're moving forward. The past is part of your history, but now – you're Starting Over Single.

SOS – Let's begin.

Tip # 1: Let Yourself Grieve

Sometimes we move into the after-life of divorce or widowhood by gritting our teeth, marching forward and doing whatever we can to survive. But grief has a way of revisiting us.

If we don't grieve every loss, then bundles of pain build up over time and cause stress, dis-ease and even death.

Our Grief Minister at GateWay of Hope describes bundled-up grief with a bunch of Legos. For each grief, pile one Lego on top of another one. You might create a colorful design but it won't be long until one more Lego becomes just too much.

The entire pile falls over. That's a visual of how grief can add up and cause problems.

So right from the beginning, let's deal with your grief and let it go.

Grab a tissue. Eat some chocolate and take some time to grieve what has happened to you. Beat up a box with a baseball bat. Let the anger out. Write your emotions in your journal. Confide in a friend.

Release the pain and let yourself grieve.

Action Points:

► What have you done so far to deal with your grief?

► Do you have a professional counselor, a pastor, a coach or an accountability partner to help you process your grief? Who is that person?

► When you look back six months, how have you moved forward? How have you dealt with grief?

- ▶ Write down a favorite quote, Bible passage or thought that helps you grieve in a healthy way.

- ▶ Write down some good memories about the person or the circumstance before divorce, death or the break-up of your relationship.

- ▶ List 5 things for which you are grateful.

Tip # 2: Use Your Journal

A journal is one of the easiest and cheapest forms of therapy.

Buy yourself a notebook you like and put today's date on the first page. Or if you like to work electronically, design your own journal online.

Then start writing about how you feel.

If you don't like to write sentences and paragraphs, draw pictures. If you don't like to draw, do a webbing where you just put down words – then more words under those words. If you don't like webbings, cut pictures and words out of a magazine and glue them into your journal.

Get the emotions out of your soul and onto the paper. When you feel down-hearted, take your journal to a coffee shop or an outdoor gazebo or any place where you feel peaceful. Talk to yourself, using your journal.

Commit to writing in your journal on a regular basis. This doesn't have to be a daily chore. You can use your journal every other day, M-W-F, once per week, twice per month. It's up to you.

Just do it. Start now.

Action Points:

Journal about these thoughts:

- ▶ Today, I am angry about...

- ▶ When I think about what happened to me, I just want to...

- ▶ Even though I don't understand all of this, I feel that...

▶ One thing I am grateful for is…

▶ I'm letting the old dreams go, and my new dream is…

Now, don't you feel better already?

Tip # 3: Read Isaiah 54

The Bible has a wealth of wisdom, and Isaiah 54 is particularly wonderful for women who are Starting Over Single.

Isaiah was a prophet who lived thousands of years ago. He wrote about things which were to come in the future, but his words also apply to us today.

Some of Isaiah's ideas in Chapter 54 include:

- Don't be afraid
- Be strong
- Don't feel ashamed or humiliated
- God loves you, and He still has a good plan for you
- God cares about how you feel
- God will take care of your children
- If anyone comes against you, it won't be from God

So go ahead and read the entire chapter, then journal about what you've learned. You may want to read it every day for a week and search for some nuggets of hope each time you read it.

You might also read it in several different versions so that you can understand it even better.

Action Points:

► What was your favorite verse in Isaiah 54?

► Why was this your favorite verse?

► How does God show you that he cares about you?

▶ How are you stronger now than you were at the beginning of your SOS journey?

▶ What other Bible passages have helped you Start Over Single?

▶ What other books have helped you Start Over Single?

Tip # 4: Exercise

Yeah, I know. We don't always like to exercise, but it really *is* one of the best tips for moving forward.

Find some kind of exercise that you enjoy enough to do every day. Exercise will help you think more clearly and it will help you to keep off those extra pounds that might hamper you in finding a job and staying healthy.

Exercise will also release endorphins that fight against depression. Nobody wants to live with depression.

You don't need fancy equipment, and you don't have to buy a membership in a gym. But if you want to invest in these things and they fit into your budget – go ahead.

Whatever you do, just get moving. Even if it's only 10 minutes/day, do some kind of exercise.

Action Points:

► Ride a stationary bike.

► Run in place.

► Walk around your neighborhood.

► Grab a friend and do a dance together.

► Watch a workout DVD and follow what they tell you to do.

► Take a break every hour – get away from the computer, stand up and stretch.

► Find a yoga DVD at the Half Price Store.

- ▶ Use your lunch hour to walk around the building.

- ▶ Find a building in your area that has several flights of stairs. Run up the stairs for 30 minutes.

- ▶ Do a prayer walk around your neighborhood. This exercises physical *and* spiritual muscles.

- ▶ Make exercise a family activity.

- ▶ Call your accountability partner / coach and tell her how you exercised today.

Tip # 5: Join a Support Group

It is always helpful to know we are not alone, so finding some type of support group is essential for moving forward.

At GateWay of Hope, we offer our SOS group every fall and every spring – 15 weeks of a group coaching format to learn more about budgets, self-care, parenting, etc.

Maybe a support group exists in your town or in your church. If not, start one yourself. Get together for a few snacks and some girlfriend time. Share best practices. Go through this booklet together.

Check out the churches that offer Divorce Care™. This is the first line of defense as you Start Over Single. First Divorce Care; then SOS.

Women are particularly wise in finding ways to help each other. We know how to relate and how to nurture.

This is the time for you to draw even closer to your friends, but beware. Some of your married friends will disconnect from you. That's okay. This is not your fault. They don't understand.

Strength *does* lie in numbers and we need to be in community with each other. So grab your purse and drive to the nearest support group.

Action Points:

► List below the names of the women you feel you can trust.

► Make a coffee appointment to meet one of them within the next two weeks.

► Be honest about what you need your friends to do for you:

    ○ Help you figure out a budget
    ○ Give you a generous hug
    ○ Keep you accountable so that you will exercise
    ○ Help you network for a better job
    ○ Pray for you daily
    ○ Help you make inexpensive Christmas gifts for your children
    ○ Go shopping with you

► Make a note on your calendar to check into a local support group.

Tip # 6: Laugh

What you've been through is far from funny, but laughter is good for the soul. We need to find the humor in every situation and practice joy.

Laughter is also good for the body. Scientific studies reveal the fact that laughter and a positive attitude help us stay physically healthy.

But how can you possibly laugh when you're Starting Over Single?

You can laugh if you work at it, and if you put humorous things and people into your life.

Just make a point of trying to find the humor in every situation.

Action Points:

- Check out a funny DVD from the library.

- Read a joke book.

- Buy one of those laughing toys.

- Spend time with children.

- Check out internet sites that have funny videos.

- Rent or borrow "I Love Lucy" videos or "The Carol Burnett Show."

- Find a friend who has a great sense of humor and have coffee together.

- Stay away from toxic people.

- Cuddle with a puppy.

- Sign up for a funny webinar.

▶ Look in the mirror and make funny faces at yourself.

▶ Remind yourself to smile.

▶ Watch a PBS special starring Victor Borga.

▶ Go somewhere alone and make yourself laugh. Come on, you really *can* do it. Just let yourself go and laugh.

Tip # 7: Make Sleep a Priority

Yes, I know you're working several jobs and/or you're a single mom and you have all the responsibilities with the kids.

But your health is important and sleep is one of the components of self-care.

Most healthcare experts suggest 7-8 hours of sleep each night. Some of us need closer to nine hours. You know what is best for you.

At the beginning of the SOS journey, you may be worried about finances and insomnia might be a regular companion.

But you can work against those worries and help yourself relax so that you can truly rest.

What you didn't finish today, you can start on first tomorrow.

Set a healthy boundary for yourself and go to bed.

Sleep. Dream. Make it a priority.

Action Points:

- ▶ Take a bubble bath with lavender.

- ▶ Drink a cup of chamomile tea.

- ▶ Read Psalm 46 and ask God to help you, "Be still and know that He is God."

- ▶ On Sundays, allow yourself the pleasure of a nap. If you need a reminder, read this blog post: http://rjthesman.net/2013/11/05/rejuvenate-with-the-holy-nap/

- ▶ Read a story to your children before bed. This will help all of you to relax.

- ▶ No caffeine and no food after 7pm.

- ▶ Spend some time journaling.

- ▶ Tell yourself, "Goodnight."

- ▶ Sing a lullaby.

- ▶ Do some deep breathing exercises.

Tip # 8: Fill Your Body with Healthy Foods / Drinks

Although you might feel like eating a carton of ice cream, stuffing your mouth with sugary treats will not help you move forward.

We all know that trashy, processed food causes junk to build up in our bodies. Junk drinks do the same.

You need to stay healthy for this next phase of your life, and you need to protect the one body God has given you.

When we're Starting Over Single, we need to be able to think clearly about finances, parenting, job choices, etc. Eating junk food will affect our brains and our thinking abilities.

We also need to stay healthy so that we can do well at our jobs and have more energy to take care of our children.

Stress affects the cortisol in our bodies and can cause us to gain weight. Most women who Start Over Single, either gain excess weight or stop eating regularly and lose too much weight. Both of these scenarios are unhealthy.

Commit to a healthy food plan and follow the action points below. You'll feel better and you'll move forward with a healthier body and a happier attitude.

You only get one body. Take care of it.

Action Points:

► Delete high fructose corn syrup from your diet.

► Consider the sodas and other sugary drinks in your diet. Yes, that includes diet drinks which may actually have more harmful chemicals than regular sugary drinks.

- ▶ Drink high quality water and maybe a little coffee or tea – the real stuff – not the flavored kind.

- ▶ A tiny bit of dark chocolate is good for you, but not all the time.

- ▶ Shop the outer areas of the grocery store where all the produce is kept. Eat organic.

- ▶ Make it your habit to follow the Mediterranean diet which is one of the healthiest lifestyle changes you can make: fresh vegetables and fruits, chicken, fish, extra virgin olive oil, whole grains and nuts.

- ▶ Avoid fast food. It costs more than cooking at home and in the long-run, it may eventually trash your body.

- ▶ Eat all your meals on a small plate or in a small bowl. When you eat less, you'll feel better and sleep better.

- ▶ Don't eat after 7pm. This will help you with Tip # 7. You'll sleep better.

- ▶ Shop in a natural foods store or in your local farmer's market.

Tip # 9: Treat Yourself to Some Fun

You've been through a major life crisis, and everything has been difficult.

So...you need to have some fun. Even if it's just once / month – plan for some fun time.

The first step is to realize that it's okay to have fun. You deserve it. You've worked hard at your job(s), you've worked with attorneys and financial advisors and you've been through a lot of grief. You may have struggled through a harrowing and disastrous marriage for many years.

Give yourself permission to have some fun, but make sure it's healthy fun. Nobody needs to schedule a hangover in their planner.

Try some of these fun ideas. You'll feel better when you do.

Action Points:

- ▶ Schedule a Day of Joy in your planner.

- ▶ Go to a lawn and garden center and revel in the flowers.

- ▶ Find a cheap matinee and go see a movie and yes – eat the popcorn.

- ▶ Join a friend for lunch and share a BOGO coupon.

- ▶ Soak in a tub of lavender bubbles.

- ▶ Get a manicure / pedicure at the beauty school.

- ▶ Browse through a cozy bookstore.

- ▶ Take a leisurely drive into the country.

▶ Spend some time at a petting zoo.

▶ Get out your colors and finish a page in your coloring book.

▶ Bake chocolate chip cookies with a friend.

▶ Walk through the crunchy autumn leaves.

▶ Make a snow angel.

▶ Come up with your own list and circle dates in your calendar for fun.

Tip # 10: Remember that Healing Takes Time

Nobody immediately bounces back from a divorce, a death or the break-up of a relationship. Healing takes time.

Don't try to recover too fast or force yourself to smile and pretend that life is wonderful.

You were together for a long time. It takes a while to get over that type of loss.

Divorce Care™ suggests one year of healing for every four years of marriage. This is a general guideline, and each woman heals at her own rate.

Grief looks different for each of us. It does not come with a formula or a default timeline.

If you are constantly talking about the relationship, the divorce, the death – that is an indication that you still need to heal.

Forgiveness is a process and part of the journey. When we refuse to forgive, we sabotage our healing process. But each of us forgives at a different rate, too.

So…give yourself time to heal. Give yourself grace.

Action Points:

▶ Get plenty of rest. Healing takes a lot of energy. See Tip # 7.

▶ Consider professional counseling to help you work through the hurting places. If you're in the Kansas City area, call GateWay of Hope at 913.393.4283; www.GWHope.org

▶ Talk to your pastor or a trusted spiritual advisor.

- Journal about your feelings and date each journal entry. In six months, go back and read some of your past entries. You'll see your own growth happening on the page.

- Do some type of creative project that gives you joy: paint one of the rooms in your house, design and sew a quilt for a friend, compose a song, write a story, make some jewelry, etc.

- Spend time in nature. Walk and talk to God.

- Rescue a pet that will love you unconditionally.

- Spend extra time with family and friends. Let your support system love you.

- Find a grief support group. Check out any organizations that have special grief supports to cope with the holidays.

Tip # 11: Follow the One Year Rule

This tip goes along with Tip # 10. When you're Starting Over Single, it takes a while to get your brains back and the clarity you will need for major decisions.

Give yourself at least one year to heal – one year before you make any major decisions.

- One year before you sell the house, unless it's part of the divorce settlement
- One year before you start dating again
- One year before you clean out everything and trash all the stuff that brings up memories
- One year before you move to another state or country
- One year before you look for a different job – unless you immediately need another job for survival

Impulsive decisions will backfire on you.

The nightly news is filled with stories of women in trouble – women who jumped into new relationships too soon.

You need time to find your true self again. Even if you lived in a happy marriage, you may have forgotten who you really are. You need time to just be yourself.

Jumping too soon into another relationship before you are healed will increase your chances of another divorce. You need time to heal.

Healthy women attract healthy men.

Follow the one year rule.

Action Points:

▶ Circle the date on next year's calendar that represents when the divorce was final or when the death or break-up occurred. That is your target date.

▶ Ask your accountability partner to circle the same date on her calendar. Ask her to remind you often to follow the one year rule.

▶ Tell your support group about your one year date. Ask them to help you stay accountable.

▶ If people try to fix you up for dates, remind them of your one year rule. Keep your boundaries secure.

▶ Follow the one year rule. Okay – I know we've repeated that several times, but it's important. Most of us think we're healthier than we really are. We think we can make major decisions and move forward more quickly than we should.

▶ One more time: Follow the one year rule.

Tip # 12: Wear a Tiara

Divorce affects our self-esteem and shatters our confidence. If we've been left for another person, we feel as if we're not enough – not pretty enough, not thin enough, not smart enough, etc.

That is a lie straight from hell!

The visual of a tiara helps to remind us who we really are and how wonderful life will someday be.

Go to a toy store and buy a cheap tiara, but pretend that it's made of diamonds, rubies, emeralds – all kinds of costly jewels.

Wear the tiara around the house to remind you that you have great value. You are a princess. You are highly-valued by God and by many others.

Your children think you are the greatest person who has ever walked the earth – even if they haven't told you so.

Wear the tiara when you're cleaning out toilets. It's hard to feel discouraged when you wear a tiara, even with your hands in the toilet.

Stand up tall, put on your tiara and remind yourself how wonderful you are.

Action Points:

Repeat these sentences as you look at yourself in the mirror:

- ► I am beautiful.

- ► I am greatly loved by many people and especially – by God.

- ► I have a great future ahead of me.

- As a daughter of God, I am royalty and therefore; I am worthy of respect.

- I will believe the truth and refuse any lies.

- God created me, and in his eyes, I am enough.

- I have many gifts and talents. My favorite is
_____.

- I *am* enough. In fact, I am more than enough.

- Even though I'm Starting Over Single, I'm going to make it and I'll be just fine.

Tip # 13: Ask for Help

Many people in churches and service organizations possess the gift of generosity. They love to give.

Some of these people have a special place in their hearts for the woman who is Starting Over Single.

They want to help you, but they may not know how. It is your job to tell them.

As women who are nurturers, as mothers and grandmothers who take care of others – we spend so much of our lives giving, giving and giving. It feels backward to receive.

But when we're Starting Over Single, we need to learn how to receive. It's okay to ask for help. Let me repeat that: it's okay to ask for help. No one will think poorly of you.

Don't be afraid to ask.

A day will come when you can give again. Someday, you'll be more financially secure and you'll be a giver to many causes and countless people. But right now – you need help.

So go ahead. Ask for help.

Action Points:

► Go to your pastor or to the leader of a service organization and ask for what you need. Many service organizations are especially helpful, and they will often give you a list for resources.

- ▶ A bed for your child? Ask.
- ▶ New tires for your car? Ask.
- ▶ Someone to help you with plumbing, electrical work, house-cleaning, lawn work? Ask.

- ▶ You need a bookcase in your office so you can work more effectively? Ask.
- ▶ Thanksgiving is coming and you can't afford a turkey. Ask.
- ▶ You need a haircut so you can feel confident for that job interview. Ask.

- ▶ You're putting the house on the market and you need help to paint the rooms. Ask.
- ▶ Your microwave just blasted its last wave, and you can't afford a new one. Ask.
- ▶ The kitchen sink gasket has broken and water squirts everywhere. Ask.

People don't know how to help if you don't ask.

They may say, "No," and that's okay. At least you tried.

But they can't say, "Yes," unless you ask.

Tip # 14: Consider Professional Counseling / Coaching

Many professionals are highly-skilled in helping women who are Starting Over Single.

At GateWay of Hope, I am a life coach who specializes in this niche. I can help you with your budget, your individualized plan for how to move forward and any number of important topics. I can also Skype with you for coaching sessions. You don't have to live in Kansas City. Check out the GateWay of Hope website at: www.GWHope.org

Many counselors possess the skills and experience to help you through your grief process. They can show you why it's important not to live in shame or false guilt. They can point out the importance of expressing your anger, then forgiving that person who hurt you so deeply.

It is no disgrace to seek counseling and/or coaching. Professionals want to help you, and they have the skills to do that.

Yes, it costs something, but when you begin to thrive and start over with joy – the results will be worth the cost.

Many nonprofit organizations charge for their services with a sliding scale, dependent on your budget. Others provide scholarships so that women can take advantage of counseling and/or coaching. Even some of our groups at GateWay of Hope offer scholarships.

Don't let the cost deter you from emotional and mental health.

You have been through a life-changing event that affects every part of your personhood – body, soul and spirit.

Professionals can help you deal with the past and move forward with confidence.

Action Points:

- ▶ Begin with your pastor and ask him/her for counseling resources.

- ▶ Make an appointment this week with a counselor or a coach.

- ▶ Fill out this statement: My appointment is _____ and I will be there on time.

- ▶ Remind yourself that you are moving forward in life and this is a necessary step.

- ▶ Buy a journal that you will use specifically for your counseling / coaching.

- ▶ Consider Proverbs 11:14, "Where there is no guidance, the people fall, but in abundance of counselors there is victory."

"The journey of a thousand miles begins with a single step." – Lao-tzu

Tip # 15: Take Care of Your Health

Self-care is not selfish, and the stress of Starting Over Single can impact your overall health.

Taking care of yourself is vital as you journey forward. To make it to the finish line, you will need overall health.

If you're a single Mom, your children need you to be healthy. A perfect example comes to us from the airlines. If the oxygen masks come down, Mom needs to put one on herself first so that she can help her children. If Mom passes out, everyone suffers.

Health includes more than the physical aspect. Taking care of yourself includes the emotional, mental and spiritual parts of you. All of these have been affected by the divorce, the death or the break-up. All of these parts need to be healthy in order to move forward.

Action Points:

- ► Physical
    - o Schedule your annual physical. If you can't afford health insurance, then find a clinic that offers free mammograms and Pap smears.
    - o Tell your doctor about any health concerns and follow your doctor's advice.
    - o Dental health is important because oral health affects other areas of our bodies. Find a clinic or a dental school that offers free cleanings. Keep regular dental appointments.
    - o Floss and brush. Stay away from sugary treats and sodas.
    - o Avoid processed foods.
    - o Exercise. Even 10 minutes/day of walking in place will help you feel better.
    - o Take a good multi-vitamin. Calcium and vitamin D are also important for women.

- ▶ Emotional / Mental
  - ○ Do something fun once / week.
  - ○ Find a support group to belong to.
  - ○ Journal.
  - ○ Pull out your colors and coloring book. Coloring is a great stress reliever.
  - ○ Take walks at a nature center.
  - ○ Call an old friend and share a coffee.
  - ○ Schedule a Day of Joy – an art gallery, garden nursery, music store, bookstore, etc.
  - ○ Check out some of the courses at the community college. Learn a new language.

- ▶ Spiritual
  - ○ Take your journal outdoors and write 10 thank you's to God.
  - ○ Join a women's Bible study.
  - ○ Observe the Sabbath and take a holy nap.
  - ○ Join a book club.
  - ○ Schedule time for God in your planner – talk to Him and listen.
  - ○ Play some praise music and lift your heart to God.
  - ○ Read a poem or compose your own poem about God's love for you.
  - ○ Every night before bed, read a Psalm. Every morning, read a Proverb.

Tip # 16: Contact a Professional about Finances

Even if you're a whiz kid with dollars, it's possible to be tricked by con artists who think single women are easy prey. Everybody wants your money, and you need to be on guard for any types of get-rich schemes.

As we're Starting Over Single, most of us take a financial hit. We may lose the house and often, the primary income. We have to return to work or find a second and maybe a third job. We pinch pennies, use coupons and save everything we can.

Once the shock wears off, we think it's time to buy another house or move to another section of town, another state – even another country.

But some of those choices aren't financially smart. It's wise to talk to a financial professional or even a good friend who is good with finances – someone who is objective and can tell you the truth. You are now responsible for your own financial health.

Action Points:

- ► Find a professional you trust and be frank about your budget.

- ► Keep track of everything you spend for one month – everything – every single penny. This will give you an idea of which categories you need to consider in your budget.

- ► Consider your relationship to money:
    - o Are you afraid to deal with it?
    - o Do you need a certain amount to feel secure?
    - o What were the emotions toward money in your marriage? Were they healthy?

- ► Don't buy anything impulsively just to make yourself feel better.

- Be careful and be smart. Save for the long run and don't try to recover too fast.

- Save a little bit – even a dollar – from every paycheck.

- Keep a picture of something you really want: a vacation, a new car, a different house. Then save for that item.

- Enlist the help of your family. Keep a change jar. At the end of every week, everyone puts their change in the jar. This will become your Christmas money.

- Follow a budget plan whether it's online or in hard copy.

- Be ruthless in cutting expenses which is easier than finding another income.

Tip # 17: Memorize Psalm 43:5 NIV

"Hope in God for I will **YET** praise Him, my Savior and my God."

When you memorize Bible verses, they help you focus on the positive and fight against discouragement.

Learning Bible verses also helps to cement your core values.

It's important to stay in hope, every moment of every day. Hope *does* exist and some day – your life will be so different – you'll be amazed.

Live in the **YET**. This is the place you're headed for and by believing that life can be better, you will consistently move forward. You won't get stuck in the past or be overwhelmed by fear.

Live in what is **YET** to come – a better life, new dreams that will come true, maybe even a new and better relationship.

Stay in Hope and Live in the **YET**.

Action Points:

▶ Find a favorite Bible verse that meets your current need. If you need some ideas, check out these verses below:

"Why are you in despair, O my soul? And why are you disturbed within me? Hope in God, for I shall again praise Him, the help of my countenance, and my God." Psalm 43:5 NASB

"The LORD your God is with you, the Mighty Warrior who saves. He will take great delight in you; in his love he will no longer rebuke you, but will rejoice over you with singing." Zephaniah 3:17 NIV

"I sought the Lord, and He answered me, and delivered me from all my fears." Psalm 34:4 NASB

"The thief comes only to steal and kill and destroy. I came that they may have life and have it abundantly." John 10:10 ESV

"My soul, wait in silence for God only, for my hope is from Him. He only is my rock and my salvation, my stronghold; I shall not be shaken." Psalm 62:5-6 NASB

► Write the verse you like on a 3 x 5 card and carry it with you.

► Review it several times each day. Soon, you will have it memorized and you will think about it often.

► Journal about how your particular verse gives you hope.

Tip # 18: Let God Love You

God never rejects us or betrays us. He is our greatest lover, because he doesn't request anything of us – except to love him back.

Isaiah expressed this truth: "For your husband is your Maker" (Isaiah 54:5).

Jesus is the one person we can depend on to be our Heavenly Husband. We can talk to him every day and know he will never let us down. He is faithful. He doesn't betray his promises.

Do we ever get lonely for physical affection? Of course. But even then, we can tell Jesus that we love him and we need him to show up. We need him to give us a spiritual hug.

> Sometimes he shows up in a friend or even in a stranger who is kind to us.

> Sometimes he shows up with a surprise package in the mail or an extra check that meets a current need.

> Sometimes he does something so unusual and wonderful, we call it a "Godwink."

God has a special place in his heart for the orphan and the widow. This verse applies to women and children who are abandoned and vulnerable. Women of divorce are also considered widows.

God will answer your prayers and send love notes, Godwinks, to you. Get ready to receive.

Let God love you.

Action Points:

▶ Make a special place in your journal to record the Godwinks that happen to you.

▶ Share these Godwinks with a friend.

▶ Be alert each day for something special to happen. Record it in your journal and whisper a prayer of thanks.

▶ Teach your children to watch for Godwinks. This will help all of you be more aware of the encouragements God sends.

▶ Be honest with God. When you're feeling lonely or especially vulnerable, tell him. He will know how to respond best to you and meet your need.

▶ Start every morning with the statement, "God, I love you." Then listen for his love reply back to you.

▶ Remember Philippians 4:19, *"And my God shall supply all your needs according to His riches in glory in Christ Jesus."*

Tip # 19: Celebrate Every Victory

If you've been following all of these tips, you've come a long way.

Celebrate your progress!

When you make it through a difficult day, celebrate who you are.

You persevered. You succeeded. Good for you!

Action Points:

▶ When you pay the bills, celebrate because you know how to do that and you're moving forward financially.

▶ When you refuse to live in anger or revenge, celebrate that joy. You're a better person for it.

▶ When you feel as if you've forgiven another piece of the hurt, celebrate by thanking God.

▶ Look back every few months and read through your journal entries. Look at how you've grown! You're an amazing woman.

▶ Tell one of your friends about how you've moved past another milestone.

▶ Once/month, treat yourself to something special: a piece of dark chocolate, a new bracelet, a pretty scarf.

▶ Look in the mirror and smile at yourself. You've done it, and God has been loving you throughout this process.

▶ You're stronger than ever before and even if life is hard – it is better than it was.

▶ Celebrate you!

So we've made it to the end of the 19 Tips. Hurray!

You've made some amazing progress and you're learning how to live in hope.

I would love to celebrate with you.
Contact me at: rebeccat@GWHope.org

Helpful Resources:

Isaiah 54   Psalm 62
Philippians 4   Psalm 34
Psalm 43   John 10
Zephaniah 3   Psalm 27

Books:

"Safe People" by Dr. Henry Cloud and Dr. John Townsend

"Boundaries" by Dr. Henry Cloud and Dr. John Townsend

"How Not to Date a Loser" by Georgia Shaffer

"Singles Ask" by Harold Ivan Smith

"Suddenly Single" by Jim Smoke

"Forty Something and Single" by Harold Ivan Smith

"9 Things You Simply Must Do to Succeed in Love and Life" by Dr. Henry Cloud

"Every Single Day" by Donna Huisjen

Websites:

www.**GWHope.org** (GateWay of Hope)

www.**DivorceCare.org** (Divorce Care)

www.**daveramsey.com** (Financial Peace University)

www.**crown.org** (Crown Financial Ministries)

www.**debtproofliving.com** (Debt-Proof Living)

www.**EmergeVictorious.com** (Emerge Victorious)

www.**soulfast.com** (The 40 Day Soul Fast; Your Journey to Authentic Living)

www.**cloudtownsend.com** (Boundaries)

www.**midlifedivorcerecovery.com** (Midlife Divorce Recovery – Kansas City)

Made in the USA
Coppell, TX
05 July 2022

79595163R00024